DIGGING INTO HISTORY

SOLVING THE MYSTERIES OF
THE PYRAMIDS

Fiona MacDonald

This paperback edition published in 2014
by Franklin Watts
338 Euston Road
London NW1 3BH

Franklin Watts Australia
Level 17/207 Kent Street
Sydney, NSW 2000

A CIP catalogue record for this book
is available from the British Library.

ISBN: 978 1 4451 3440 6

Dewey no. 932

Printed in China

Franklin Watts is a division of
Hachette Children's Books,
an Hachette UK company.
www.hachette.co.uk

Note to parents and teachers concerning
websites: In the book every effort has been
made by the Publishers to ensure that
websites are suitable for children, that they
are of the highest educational value, and that
they contain no inappropriate or offensive
material. However, because of the nature of
the Internet, it is impossible to guarantee that
the contents of these sites will not be altered.
We advise that Internet access is supervised
by a responsible adult.

Designer: Dave Allen
Picture Researcher: Clare Newman
Managing Editor: Tim Cooke
Indexer: Kay Ollerenshaw
Editorial Director: Lindsey Lowe

Picture Credits
The photographs in this book are used by
permission and through the courtesy of:

Front cover: Galyna Andrushko/ Shutterstock

Alamy: Panacea Pictures 29, Ivor Toms 9;
Bridgeman Art Library: Aegyptsches Museum 24,
British Museum 1, 7, 15, Egyptian Museum 19,
22, Peter Willi 12; Corbis: Dave Bartruft 26-27,
Gianni Dagli Orti 25, Hulton Deutsch 21, Carl &
Ann Purcell 8, Reuters 28br, Stapleton Collection
20, Supreme Council of Antiquities 18, Sandra
Vannin 16, Ron Watts 17t; Mary Evans Picture
Library: 23; PA Photos: Ben Curtis/AP 14, Alfred de
Montesquiou/AP 27; Shutterstock: Albo 6b, Styve
Reineck 10-11, Sculpies 4-5, Russell Shively 6t, 13,
Paul Vorwerk 17b; Tophoto: Charles Walker 28bl.

Contents

WHAT IS THE SECRET OF THE PYRAMIDS?

MASSIVE, MAGNIFICENT, MYSTERIOUS... THE PYRAMIDS OF EGYPT ARE ONE OF THE GREAT WONDERS OF THE WORLD. BUT WHY WERE THEY BUILT?

The **pyramids** are tombs. **Pharaohs**, kings of ancient Egypt, were buried inside the pyramids from around 2600 to 1800 BCE. More than ninety pyramids still survive today. Most stand near Memphis, Egypt's first capital city, on the west bank of the River Nile.

The Egyptians believed that the west bank of the Nile was the land of the dead, haunted by ghosts and scavenging jackals. The pyramids are surrounded by groups of temples and smaller tombs.

Pyramids were also **sacred** places. The Egyptians believed that their land was blessed by the gods. They saw the pyramid as a stairway that helped the dead pharaoh reach heaven. The shape was also a symbol of the rays of the Sun. Egyptians thought that dead pharaohs lived in the sky with Ra, the Sun god.

Some pyramid temples sheltered the pharaoh's body before burial. Others stored offerings to help pharaohs in the **afterlife**. These temples were also important for

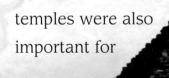

the living. The temple complex included farms that employed many workers. The priests were advisors to the government.

WHAT'S INSIDE?

The pyramids have long inspired curiosity. The first **excavations** near a pyramid were ordered by Pharaoh Tuthmosis IV as early as 1400 BCE. He removed the desert sand that had buried the Great **Sphinx** – a giant statue with a lion's body and a human face that guards Pharaoh Khafre's pyramid at Giza.

From around 400 BCE to 300 CE, visitors from Greece and Rome came to see Egypt. After Arabs conquered Egypt in 642 CE, Muslims from Asia and Africa visited the ruins. Around 820 CE, the caliph, or Islamic leader, al-Mamun, tried to crack open the Great Pyramid at Giza by lighting fires on it and then pouring cold vinegar on its stones. **Crusaders** also passed through Egypt on their way to the Holy Land.

SCHOLARS AND SCOUNDRELS

Around the 1500s, European **scholars** began to visit Egypt. They published accounts of their trips that got more people interested in Egypt. In the 1600s, the German scholar Athanasius Kircher unsuccessfully tried to decipher the picture writing, or **hieroglyphs**, that appeared inside the pyramids and on other ancient Egyptian **monuments**.

LEFT: *The Great Pyramid at Giza (right), built for Khufu around 2589 BCE, is the largest pyramid: 146 metres (480 feet) tall with a base that covers over 5.3 hectares (13 acres).*

SOLVING THE MYSTERIES OF THE PYRAMIDS

In 1798 the French general Napoleon Bonaparte invaded Egypt. He sent 150 artists and engineers to survey all its monuments. Their findings, published between 1809 and 1822, brought more European and American visitors. Some travellers made valuable discoveries, but others did great harm. One Englishman even used dynamite in his excavations. Others were only interested in finding treasure to sell to museums. Tourists, including the US writer Mark Twain and British heroine Florence Nightingale,

ABOVE: *A carving with picture writing, or hieroglyphs. When scholars began studying ancient Egypt, no one had been able to read hieroglyphs for over 1,500 years.*

BELOW: *The Great Sphinx at Giza is the best known of many statues of the part-human, part-lion monster that traditionally protected Egypt from its enemies.*

unintentionally damaged monuments. Visitors rode on horseback through temples and climbed up the pyramids.

COORDINATED EFFORTS

In 1851, when the Turks ruled Egypt, they appointed French expert August Mariette to oversee excavations and protect the ruins. In the 1880s, Egyptologists led by Flinders Petrie (from England) and George Reisner (from the United States) pioneered scientific excavation. Today, all excavations are run by Egypt's Supreme **Antiquities** Council. Even after centuries of research, exciting discoveries are still being made.

ABOVE: The three written languages on the Rosetta Stone gave codebreakers the clues they needed to crack the meaning of the hieroglyphs.

The Rosetta Stone

Ancient Egyptians used hieroglyphs mainly for sacred purposes. Carved and painted hieroglyphs listed the achievements of the pharaohs or appeared as prayers, hymns or spells inside pyramids. For everyday use, Egyptians used a simpler, quicker style of writing called demotic ('everyday').

In 1799 a French soldier repairing a fort found a black stone slab at el-Rashid (Rosetta) in Egypt. It was carved around 180 BCE with the same written passage in three scripts: hieroglyphs, demotic and ancient Greek. Scholars could understand the Greek and compare it with the other two scripts. The hieroglyphs were so complicated that it took more than twenty years before a young French genius named Jean-François Champollion cracked the code.

Tomb Robbers

Tombs full of valuable treasure were targets for robbers. By 1000 BCE **looters** had broken into nearly all of Egypt's pyramids. The robbers were not stopped by defences such as dead-ends, dummy chambers, false doors, pits, booby traps and magic spells. Looters probably threatened or bribed tomb builders to get inside.

The robbers stripped off golden masks from **mummies** and gold leaf from coffins. They stole jewels, weapons, clothes and furniture. They even tore mummies apart to find the precious **charms** hidden inside their linen wrappings.

?

DID YOU KNOW

In 1881 experts investigated tomb robbers selling ancient treasure – and found forty mummies, including that of Ramses II.

BELOW: *Many Egyptian tombs, like this one in the Valley of the Kings, were looted soon after they were built. Thousands of years later, looting is still a problem.*

By around 1500 BCE, the problem of looting had become so bad that some pharaohs chose to be buried in hidden tombs, not pyramids, in an area called the Valley of the Kings. But even there, they were not safe from discovery.

PROTECTIVE MEASURES

Tomb robbing continued throughout Egypt's long history. Rulers, tourists and invaders, as well as poor villagers and professional thieves, destroyed many parts of Egypt's great heritage.

ABOVE: *This obelisk from the reign of Pharaoh Ptolemy VII was looted in 1821 and erected in the grounds of Kingston Lacy house, Dorset.*

Today the unlawful transport or sale of ancient **artefacts** is forbidden by international conventions. Governments have also passed laws to punish looters and smugglers. Many countries, including Egypt, have organisations responsible for protecting national treasures. Museums, galleries, art dealers and police forces have set up information networks to record stolen objects and help catch the looters.

WHO BUILT THE PYRAMIDS?

FOR MORE THAN THREE THOUSAND YEARS EGYPT WAS HOME TO A RICH AND SPLENDID CIVILISATION WHOSE RULERS CREATED SPECTACULAR MONUMENTS.

Egypt's ruins give fascinating glimpses of the civilisation that created them. Along the Nile the pharaohs built temples, statues, palaces and pyramids. **Archaeologists** have unearthed other wonderful signs of Egypt's past: glass, pottery, jewellery, weapons, paintings, clothing, musical instruments and toys. They have found **scrolls** of papyrus – a paper made from reeds – containing poems, stories and lists of laws. The texts reveal what the Egyptians knew about astronomy, mathematics and medicine.

THE RIVER OF LIFE

The wealth to create all of the treasures came from Egypt's rich farmland. Nearly 90 per cent of Egypt was desert. But each summer, the River Nile overflowed its banks. The flood left a layer of thick, black mud. Around 5500 BCE, Egyptians began to grow wheat and barley in the fertile soil. They also dug ditches to carry water to their fields and ponds to store flood water. Egyptians believed that the mud was a magic symbol of rebirth.

FOOD FOR ALL

Farmers gave a share of their produce to the pharaohs. If they had anything left over, farmers took it to market. They traded it for goods such as pottery, baskets and blankets.

Women sold homemade linen, plus the brown bread and thick beer that were

LEFT: *The dusty cliffs of the desert rise behind a narrow strip of fields and palm trees that line the banks of the River Nile.*

Egyptian Timeline

Historians divide Egyptian history into periods. The labels can be useful – but most changes in Egyptian life happened gradually, rather than on specific dates.

5500–3100 BCE	PRE-DYNASTIC PERIOD
3100–2686 BCE	EARLY DYNASTIC PERIOD
2686–2181 BCE	OLD KINGDOM
2181–2055 BCE	FIRST INTERMEDIATE PERIOD
2055–1650 BCE	MIDDLE KINGDOM
1650–1550 BCE	SECOND INTERMEDIATE PERIOD
1550–1099 BCE	NEW KINGDOM
1069–747 BCE	THIRD INTERMEDIATE PERIOD
747–332 BCE	LATE PERIOD
332–30 BCE	PTOLEMAIC PERIOD
30 BCE–395 CE	ROMAN PERIOD

the main part of the Egyptian diet. The bread was gritty and the beer was sugary – even royal mummies have worn and rotten teeth. Other basic foods included fish from the Nile, dried beans and fruit and vegetables. Meat was a luxury for rich families only.

A RIVER HIGHWAY

People, grain and goods were all carried by boats along the Nile – from Aswan in the south to Memphis and the Delta in

LEFT: *Boats made from wood or reeds were carried downstream by the current but were powered by sails or oars to travel in the opposite direction. This model boat was found in the tomb of Tutankhamen.*

the north. Models and tomb paintings show us what the boats looked like.

In 1954 archaeologists found the remains of solar barks at Giza. These boats carried pharaohs and gods in the afterlife. One boat was found in 1,224 pieces that had to be put back together like a giant jigsaw puzzle.

EVERYDAY LIFE

Excavations in towns have revealed the homes of craftworkers, merchants, priests, scribes and officials. Artists and workmen recruited by the pharaohs lived close to royal building sites. The most famous of the builders' villages, at Deir el-Medina, was excavated early in the twentieth century. Excavators found thousands of *ostraka*, pieces of broken pottery used to scribble quick notes. The ostraka preserved details of business deals, debts, court cases and even divorces, providing valuable information about everyday life in ancient Egypt.

EGYPT'S HISTORY

Egypt first became powerful around 3100 BCE, when Upper (southern) Egypt and Lower (northern) Egypt were united by the pharaoh Narmer. During the following centuries, pharaohs conquered enemy lands, traded with neighbouring peoples and sent ships to explore the east coast of Africa. Egypt's political and military power began to weaken after 1000 BCE, but Egypt remained prosperous. It became a rich prize. Many invaders tried to control Egypt before it was conquered by the Romans in 30 CE.

Moving Abu Simbel

Between 1960 and 1971, the Egyptian government built a new dam at Aswan to control the Nile floods. The dam flooded the valley behind it and created what is now Lake Nasser. The rising waters threatened many ancient sites. Teams of experts from around the world visited to make records of the monuments before they vanished.

ABOVE: *Tourists are dwarfed by the seated figures of Ramses II outside the pharaoh's temple at Abu Simbel.*

The most important monuments included the two temples at Abu Simbel, built for Ramses II and his wife Nefertari in the thirteenth century BCE. Massive statues of the pharaoh stood at the entrances of the temples.

Experts decided to move the temples. They carefully dismantled the ancient structures, numbering all of the pieces. They then moved the pieces to a safe site on higher ground and re-assembled the temples exactly as they were before.

HOW DID THE EGYPTIANS MAKE A MUMMY?

DEATH WAS A VITAL PART OF EGYPTIAN CULTURE. BODIES WERE CAREFULLY PRESERVED AND BURIED WITH SUPPLIES FOR THE AFTERLIFE.

Around 450 BCE, the Greek writer Herodotus described how Egyptians wrapped bodies in linen to make mummies. His account is very valuable. The priests and workers who handled dead bodies kept their techniques secret. Only one series of Egyptian tomb paintings shows a mummy being made.

EARLY ERRORS

Early archaeologists did not know much about **preservation**. They unwrapped mummies quickly and left few records of what they saw as they removed the bandages. French Egyptologist Gaston Maspero took just fifteen minutes to unwrap the mummy of Ramses II in

Cairo in 1886. Tutankhamen's body actually broke into pieces when it was unwrapped by Howard Carter's team in 1923.

Modern experts are more careful. In 1981, a team from the University of Bristol in the United Kingdom unwrapped the mummy of a royal official called Horemkenesi. They spent two weeks unravelling the bandages. They recorded the position of each scrap of cloth and explained how it shaped the body. They also analysed the waxes and oils rubbed into the skin and showed how they preserved the body.

MAKING A MUMMY

Modern experts have tried turning dead bodies into mummies in the way Herodotus described. They have learned that the best mummies took about ten weeks to make. First, the brain was

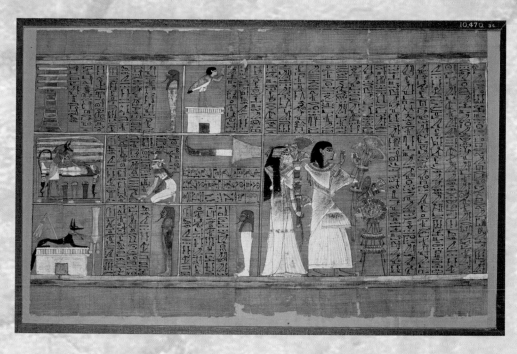

ABOVE: *This page of spells from the* Book of the Dead *includes an image of Anubis, the jackal-headed god of the dead, in the lower left-hand corner.*

LEFT: *Experts including Zahi Hawass, head of Egypt's Supreme Council of Antiquities (wearing the hat), examine the body of pharaoh Tutankhamen in 2005.*

Books of the Dead

Starting in about 1650 BCE, mummies were often buried with the *Book of the Dead*. This collection of spells was designed to help the dead person reach paradise. On the journey to paradise, the dead person's heart was weighed against a feather, the symbol of truth, to see if the person had lived a good life. If his or her heart was heavier than the feather, it was eaten by a monster.

ABOVE: *Organs removed from bodies were stored in special containers called canopic jars.*

Grave Goods

Like many ancient peoples, the Egyptians believed that life after death was similar to life on Earth. Therefore, they buried the dead with everything they might need in the afterlife: food, clothes, jewels, furniture, weapons, tools and games. The amount and quality of these grave goods varied with the wealth of the dead person. Poor farmers were buried with a few beads and cooking pots; pharaohs were surrounded by precious treasures. Grave goods are one of the most important sources of information about how people lived in the past.

Many Egyptian graves also contained model servants, called *shabtis*. Their duty was to do any work that gods and spirits in the afterlife might ask the dead person to do.

pulled out through the nose. Other organs were removed through a cut in the side. Next, the body was washed in water or wine and covered in salt from the desert. The salt soaked up water and dissolved body fat to dry the body.

After forty days, the dried body was rubbed with oil, wax and resin (gum from trees). It was packed with sand or cloth to give it a lifelike shape and then wrapped. The best mummies had twenty layers of sheets and linen bandages, all soaked in resin. Charms called amulets were put between the layers because the Egyptians believed that they provided magical protection.

Once the mummy was wrapped, its face was covered with a mask. Then the mummy was placed in one or more coffins painted with gods and magic symbols. Finally, the mummy was carried to its tomb and sealed inside a stone

sarcophagus, which served as an outer coffin. Why did the Egyptians take so much trouble to preserve the dead? The answer lies in their belief in the afterlife.

LIFE AFTER DEATH

A spell from the *Book of the Dead* explains: "You will live again, you will live forever!" The Egyptians believed that they would live in the afterlife – but only if their bodies survived. Otherwise their spirits would not be able to rejoin their bodies to enjoy an eternal life.

RIGHT: The masks that covered the faces of mummified pharaohs, like Tutankhamen's, were often made of gold, painted and decorated with precious stones.

ABOVE: Only the very wealthiest Egyptians had elaborate burials. Some mummies were simply wrapped in bandages and placed in a common tomb.

What Can We Learn from Mummies?

Mummies have not always been treated with respect. For centuries, they were ground up to create a brown paint for artists! In the 1700s and 1800s Europeans unwrapped mummies at public events simply to thrill their audiences.

SCIENTIFIC APPROACH

Scientific developments around 1900 changed the way mummies were treated. X-rays had just been invented, and some investigators began to use them to see inside mummies without unwrapping them. Other experts, led by Dr Margaret Murray from Manchester University in

?

DID YOU KNOW

Archaeologists use the same cutting-edge techniques as crime scene investigators who are trying to solve murders!

BELOW: *Zahi Hawass prepares the body of Tutankhamen for a CAT scan in 2005.*

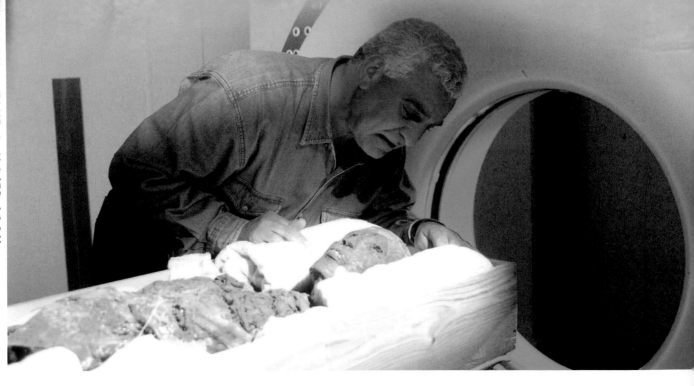

England, began to dissect mummies as if they were modern dead bodies.

Today, teams of experts with different skills work together to learn as much information as they can from mummies. They use modern technology: not just X-rays, but also electron microscopes, endoscopes (tiny cameras) and CAT scanners, which produce 3-D images of the human body.

The experts take samples of skin, flesh and bone. The samples help identify each mummy's **DNA**, or individual genetic code. Other experts analyse materials found in or around the mummy. Plant pollen, for example, can reveal what plants grew in a region at a particular time.

In this way, a team can reconstruct a mummy's whole life history. They can tell a body's age, sex, height, weight, appearance and health. They can see old injuries or the damage caused by various diseases. They can learn about the environment the person lived in – and sometimes even what his or her job was.

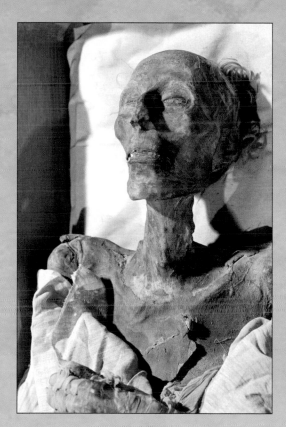

ABOVE: *A three-thousand-year-old face: The mummy of Ramses II was closely examined in 1977.*

RAMSES II

One of the most famous mummies to be subject to scientific investigation was that of Ramses II, who died in 1213 BCE. He was examined by 102 experts in Paris, France, in 1977. They found that he was unusually tall for the time – 1.68 metres (5 feet 5 inches). He had a large hooked nose, hair dyed red with henna, a nasty battle wound on one shoulder, arthritis in his hips and poor circulation in his legs. He also had a jaw abscess (infection) that must have been very painful – and that probably killed him.

WHO WAS BURIED IN THE TOMBS?

EGYPTIAN TOMBS TELL US A LOT ABOUT THE PHARAOHS THEY WERE MADE FOR – NOT JUST HOW THEY DIED, BUT ALSO HOW THEY LIVED.

When Tutankhamen's tomb was discovered by Howard Carter in 1922, its contents amazed the world. Carter's team found the famous mask that covered the dead pharaoh's face, as well as several coffins, jewellery, weapons, clothing, furniture, musical instruments and chariots – all decorated with gold or semi-precious stones.

Yet, as a pharaoh Tutankhamen achieved almost nothing. He is only famous because of his tomb. He came to power at age nine and died when he was nineteen. Most of the important

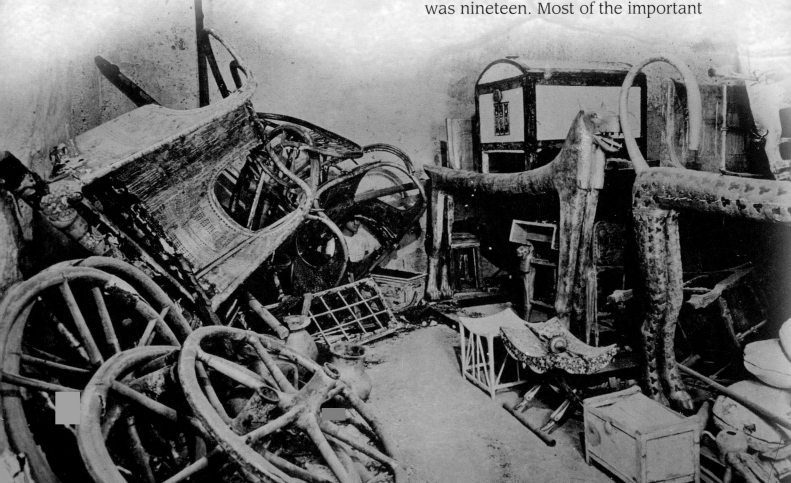

decisions during Tutankhamen's reign were probably made by government officials. But the pharaoh's magnificent burial still reveals a lot about Egypt during his reign, from 1336 to 1327 BCE.

The kingdom must have been rich and strong enough to defend its wealth from invaders. The royal family must have been highly respected or very powerful, or both, to own such treasures. The pharaoh's role as a living god must have been important to justify sending such valuable goods with him to the afterlife.

THE KING WHO WAS A QUEEN

No other tomb containing treasures equal to Tutankhamen's has been found – yet. But many pyramids, temples, statues, carvings, paintings and inscriptions from royal burials do survive and give us valuable evidence of the past.

The temple ordered by Queen Hatshepsut at Deir el-Bahri tells an extraordinary story. It is decorated with carvings showing her as the daughter of a god and wearing a false beard; Hatshepsut claimed equal powers with

LEFT: *The grave goods, including four chariots, in the tomb of Tutankhamen were found by Howard Carter in 1922.*

ABOVE: *Howard Carter crouches at the entrance of Tutankhamen's burial chamber. When asked what he could see, he replied "wonderful things".*

male pharaohs! Hatshepsut reigned from 1473 to 1458 BCE, and was one of the few women ever to rule Egypt. She came to power as regent (temporary king) because her son was too young to rule. But when he grew up, Hatshepsut did not hand over power. Instead, she carried out all the tasks of a male ruler, sending soldiers to fight in wars and ships to trade with Byblos (now in Lebanon), Sinai and East Africa. But hieroglyphs praising Hatshepsut's reign were defaced soon after she died. Some historians think that her son, Thutmose III, was trying to rewrite history. He may have wanted to make it seem as if he had never needed his mother to rule for him.

In addition to her temple, Hatshepsut also ordered a tomb in the Valley of the Kings. It has been empty for centuries – but in 2007 Hatshepsut's mummy was identified by DNA evidence and by the discovery that a tooth kept in a container bearing Hatshepsut's name fit exactly into a hole in the mummy's jawbone.

TOMBS WITHOUT BODIES

No mummy has ever been found in a pyramid, although they all contained bodies at one time. A damaged wooden coffin was found in Pharaoh Menkaura's pyramid at Giza, and a broken-off, mummified foot at Pharaoh Djoser's pyramid at Saqqara.

But pyramids can be identified by the inscriptions carved on them. Hieroglyphs at Giza proclaim "Great is Khafra" and "Menkaura is Divine". Statues inside also show how the pharaohs wanted to be remembered. Most are seated on thrones, looking stern and strong, but a few show more affectionate portraits of pharaohs and their wives, side by side.

The only known portrait of Khufu, one of Egypt's most powerful rulers, is an ivory carving 7.5 centimetres (3 inches)

LEFT: *Most portraits of pharaohs showed them as powerful rulers, but some pictured pharaohs with their wives or their families.*

Reconstructing the Past

ABOVE: *Artists' ideas of how people looked, like this 1930s portrait of Cleopatra, are still useful in creating an image of the past.*

Before the invention of the camera, archaeologists drew or painted what they found. Illustrations in newspapers and books helped spread knowledge of the past. Later, experts used photographs to record their finds. However, even a photograph only gives a flat view. Since the 1990s, digital architects have used computers to create 3-D images of ancient monuments as they would have looked when they were new. To do this, computer programs combine thousands of separate measurements of ruins. They use the data to build an image of the site and to reconstruct the likely appearance of any missing parts. The **reconstructions** enable viewers to see inside structures such as the pyramids or buried tombs — or even to walk through them.

One example of computer reconstruction, ordered by the Metropolitan Museum of Art in New York, has re-created the pyramid of Pharaoh Seworset I (reigned 1965–1920 BCE) at el-Lisht, together with all of the smaller tombs and temples around it.

23

tall. It was found by archaeologist Flinders Petrie at Abydos in the 1920s. Its tiny head was broken off, but was finally found amid heaps of stones and rubble.

A NEW PHARAOH

Occasionally, rare evidence shows us pharaohs in action. The Amarna Letters (see opposite) were mostly written to the pharaoh who ruled before Tutankhamen. Originally named Amenhotep IV, he changed his name to Akhenaten.

During his reign (1352–1336 BCE) Akhenaten tried to change traditions. He even started a new religion. Instead of honouring many gods, Akhenaten wanted Egyptians to worship only Aten, the Sun god. *Akhenaten* means 'glory of the Sun disc'. He began to build a new capital as a centre of religious power.

ABOVE: *Akhenaten commissioned realistic portrayals of himself and his wife Nefertiti, shown here in a bust supposedly by the famous sculptor Thutmose.*

Akhenaten also had artists portray him not in the usual stylised way but realistically – even his potbelly.

The Amarna Letters suggest that buildings in the new capital had no roofs. Perhaps the pharaoh wanted the citizens to feel close to Aten.

But in Egypt's hot climate, exposure to the Sun could be dangerous, and even fatal. A letter from an Assyrian ruler complains about the lack of shade: "Why are my messengers kept standing in the open Sun? They will die!"

Letters to the Pharaoh

In 1887, an Egyptian peasant gathering ancient mud bricks to break up and use as fertiliser found a heap of small clay tablets with writing on them. When they eventually reached Egyptologists, the experts realised that the tablets were letters. Most had been sent by lesser rulers and royal officials to the pharaoh Akhenaten.

The letters were written in Akkadian, the language used throughout West Asia when people from different countries needed to communicate with each other. There are about 380 Amarna Letters – named after the ruins of Akhenaten's capital city, where they

ABOVE: *Akhenaten (right) and Nefertiti worship in the rays of the god Aten, the Sun disc.*

were found. They reveal how lesser kings wrote asking the pharaoh for food during a **famine**, sent gifts to try to win his favour, agreed to trade deals and asked for help when threatened by war.

The most famous – and unusual – letter was not written to a pharaoh at all. It was sent by Queen Ankhsenpaaten, the young widow of Tutankhamen, to the king of the Hittites after the death of her teenage husband. "My husband has died," she wrote, "and I have no son... Give me one of your sons, and he might become my husband. I would not want to take [marry] one of my servants."

WHAT IS LEFT TO DISCOVER?

ALL OVER THE WORLD, BOOKS ABOUT ANCIENT EGYPT ARE BESTSELLERS, FILMS ARE BOX OFFICE HITS AND EXHIBITIONS DRAW HUGE CROWDS.

Why is ancient Egypt so fascinating? Partly because the artists, builders and craftspeople who worked there were so highly skilled. Partly because, like the ancient Egyptians, people today love the glitter of gold, the lure of mysteries and all the stories about royalty. Most of all, we like ancient Egypt because we enjoy hearing about exciting new discoveries.

Over the centuries, thousands of treasures have been found at Egyptian sites. No one knows how many more fabulous objects remain hidden. Some experts estimate that only 30 per cent of

Egypt's past has been uncovered. Experts found a previously unknown royal tomb in the Valley of the Kings in 2005 and the tomb of a royal scribe at Saqqara in 2007.

NEW VIEWS OF OLD SUBJECTS

Just as important, new techniques have revealed fresh information about even well-known monuments. Tiny cameras lowered into pits near the Giza pyramids sent back pictures of the remains of a boat that was probably used to carry a dead pharaoh to his funeral. Robots sent deep inside the Great Pyramid found a strange block of stone – perhaps a sealed door hiding a secret burial chamber.

Nearby, members of the Giza Plateau Mapping Project found the remains of a lost city that was once home to about 20,000 pyramid-builders. So far, archaeologists have found dormitories, cooking facilities, workshops and a stone coffin holding the skeleton of the city overseer.

HOW DID THE BOY KING DIE?

New techniques have also helped solve old mysteries. For example, experts have

ABOVE: *Scientists in the Valley of the Kings stand at the entrance of KV-63, a royal tomb discovered in 2005. The tomb held a series of coffins but no mummy.*

long tried to explain Tutankhamen's short reign. Since 1968, some investigators believed that he was hit in the head and murdered. In 2005, experts used a CAT scanner to make a 3-D image of Tutankhamen's body. The **CAT scan** showed that the king's skull had indeed been badly damaged – but only long after he died. The damage was probably caused when Carter's team tried to remove the pharaoh's golden mask in 1922.

LEFT: *Among the biggest threats to ancient sites are visitors who might accidentally damage them.*

Can We Have It Back?

Zahi Hawass, head of the Supreme Council of Antiquities, often campaigns for the return of ancient treasures taken from his homeland. In 2003, for example, he wrote to UNESCO asking for the return of the Rosetta Stone. Since 1802 the stone has been on display in the British Museum in London. The Egyptians argue that the Rosetta Stone, like many other artefacts, belongs to them.

Such requests can be complex, however. Museums often acquired ancient objects legally – perhaps by buying them or even by receiving them as gifts from a country's former rulers. They believe that they have a right to keep them.

The scan also showed that the young king had a badly broken thigh bone, probably caused by an accident, such as a fall from a chariot. It seems that the leg wound did not heal and the pharaoh probably died from infection.

ABOVE: *The Dendera Zodiac was once the ceiling of an Egyptian temple but was taken to France in 1821. It is one of the treasures the Egyptians want returned.*

RIGHT: *This CAT scan of Tutankhamen revealed the leg injury that may have killed the boy king.*

Archaeology is not only about exciting discoveries. It is also about preserving what has been found. For example, Egypt's Supreme Council of Antiquities has to try to protect monuments near cities from damage caused by pollution. Cars and factories produce smoke and other substances that can damage stone. Tourism is another threat. Eight million people visit Egypt every year, and most go to the pyramids. So many feet wear away the old stone. In most places, climbing on the monuments is forbidden. Grave robbing is another concern, as is the return of treasures that were taken from Egypt in the past.

ABOVE: *Tourists climb over the lower levels of a pyramid at Giza. Climbing any higher is now forbidden because the trampling of thousands of feet wears away the stones.*

DONKEY DISCOVERY

Egypt's past is still exciting and full of surprises. The largest Egyptian burial site known – the Valley of Golden Mummies at Bahariya Oasis – may contain up to 10,000 bodies from Ptolemaic and Roman Egypt, many decorated with gold. It was found by accident in 2000, when a donkey stumbled down a hole leading to one of the tombs. Such finds convince experts that there is still much to discover about the glories of ancient Egypt.

Further Resources

BOOKS

Ancient Egypt (Eyewitness). Dorling Kindersley, 2011

Fowke, Bob. *Ancient Egyptians* (What They Don't Tell You About). Wayland, 2014

Ganeri, Anita. *Great Civilisations: Egyptians*. Franklin Watts, 2014

Hewitt, Sally. *Project History: The Egyptians*. Franklin Watts, 2014

Macdonald, Fiona. *History Crafts: Ancient Egypt*. Franklin Watts, 2013

Malam, John. *History From Objects: The Egyptians*. Wayland, 2012

Minay, Rachel. *The History Detective Investigates: Ancient Egypt*. Wayland, 2014

Nilsen, Anna. *Puzzle Heroes: Ancient Egypt*. Franklin Watts, 2014

Platt, Richard. *How they made things work, The Egyptians*. Franklin Watts, 2008

Putnam, James. *Pyramid* (DK Eyewitness). Dorling Kindersley, 2004

WEB SITES

A detailed website covering many aspects of ancient Egyptian life.
http://www.bbc.co.uk/history/ancient/egyptians

The British Museum website about ancient Egypt.
http://www.ancientegypt.co.uk/

Interactive ancient Egypt pages from the Children's University of Manchester.
http://www.childrensuniversity.manchester.ac.uk/interactives/history/egypt/

The National Museum of Scotland's ancient Egypt pages.
http://www.nms.ac.uk/kids/people_of_the_past/discover_the_egyptians.aspx

Learn more about ancient Egyptian pyramids on this National Geographic website.
http://www.nationalgeographic.com/pyramids/pyramids.html

Glossary

afterlife: The place where ancient Egyptians believed the dead lived.

antiquities: Old artefacts or ruins.

archaeologist: Someone who practises the historical study of cultures by analysing remains such as artefacts and monuments.

artefact: An object that has been made or changed by humans.

CAT scan: A 3-D image of a body made by X-ray cameras and computers.

charm: An object believed to have power to protect its owner.

crusader: A Christian knight who fought the Muslim rulers of the Holy Land.

DNA: The chemical coding that passes biological information on from parents to their children.

excavation: A scientific dig to explore an archaeological site.

famine: A period of time when there is not enough food.

hieroglyphs: The symbols used instead of letters in forms of picture writing.

looters: Someone who steals treasures from old tombs, usually to sell.

monument: A structure built to celebrate a person, god or event.

mummy: A dead body that has been treated and wrapped in bandages to preserve it.

pharaoh: A ruler of ancient Egypt.

preservation: The protection of a site or object from damage.

pyramid: A four-sided structure that rises to a point.

reconstruction: An attempt to rebuild something as it looked in the past, using research and scientific data.

sacred: Something worthy of worship.

scholar: A person who studies something in great depth.

scrolls: Rolls of paper used for reading and writing.

sphinx: A monster with the body of a lion and the head of a human.

Index

Page numbers in **bold** type refer to captions.